★ ★ ★ ★ ★ ★ MILITARY FAMILIES ★ ★ ★ ★ ★ ★

My Brother Is in the
MARINE CORPS

KEISHA JONES

PowerKiDS press™

New York

Published in 2016 by The Rosen Publishing Group, Inc.
29 East 21st Street, New York, NY 10010

First Edition

Editor: Sarah Machajewski
Book Design: Katelyn Heinle

Photo Credits: Cover, pp. 5, 22 (soldier) Camille Tokerud/Taxi/Getty Images; cover backdrop, p. 1 David Smart/Shutterstock.com; pp. 3–4, 6, 8, 10, 12, 14, 16, 18, 20, 22, 24 (camouflage texture) Casper1774/Shutterstock.com; p. 7 (both) meunierd/Shutterstock.com; p. 9 (top) https://upload.wikimedia.org/wikipedia/commons/2/24/Marines01.jpg; p. 9 (bottom) https://upload.wikimedia.org/wikipedia/commons/8/8c/100329-M-6001S-166.jpg; p. 11 Ariel Skelley/Blend Images/Getty Images; p. 13 (top) ekler/Shutterstock.com; pp. 13 (bottom), 15 (bottom) Scott Olson/Getty Images News/Getty Images; p. 15 (top) Scott Olson/Photonica World/Getty Images; p. 17 (top) MLADEN ANTONOV/AFP/Getty Images; p. 17 (bottom) courtesy of U.S. Marines Flickr; p. 19 (both) ADEK BERRY/AFP/Getty Images; p. 21 Blend Images - Ariel Skelley/Brand X Pictures/Getty Images; p. 22 (American flag) Naypong/Shutterstock.com.

Library of Congress Cataloging-in-Publication Data

Jones, Keisha.
My brother is in the Marine Corps / Keisha Jones.
    pages cm. — (Military families)
Includes index.
ISBN 978-1-5081-4430-4 (pbk.)
ISBN 978-1-5081-4431-1 (6 pack)
ISBN 978-1-5081-4432-8 (library binding)
1. United States. Marine Corps—Juvenile literature. I. Title.
VE23.J65 2016
359.9'60973—dc23
                                        2015028129

Manufactured in the United States of America

CPSIA Compliance Information: Batch #BW16PK: For Further Information contact Rosen Publishing, New York, New York at 1-800-237-9932

CONTENTS

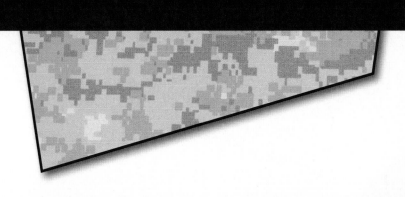

MEET MY BROTHER

    My older brother is funny, cool, and smart. He's my best friend, and he's also a marine. That means he serves in the United States Marine Corps (USMC). The United States Marine Corps is a branch of the U.S. military.

    As a marine, my brother helps **protect** the United States. He plays a part in keeping our country and its people safe. I'm proud of my brother for serving in the marines. Joining this branch of the military changed my brother's life. It changed my family's life, too. Let me tell you what it's like.

MY BROTHER'S UNIFORM HAS SPECIAL MEANING. THE MEDALS AND RIBBONS SHOW HOW HE HAS SERVED, INCLUDING WHERE HE HAS FOUGHT. HIS UNIFORM ALSO SHOWS HIS **RANK.**

THE U.S. MILITARY

The United States military has five branches. They're the Marine Corps, army, navy, coast guard, and air force. Each of these branches does something different, but they work together to do one very important job: protect and serve the United States and its citizens.

The Marine Corps is its own branch, but it belongs to the Department of the Navy. The Marine Corps and the U.S. Navy work closely together. Marines serve on navy ships and protect **naval bases**. However, the USMC is known as a "911 force" because marines are ready to **respond** to any **crisis** at a moment's notice.

MARINES ARE SOMETIMES CALLED "SOLDIERS OF THE SEA" BECAUSE OF THEIR WORK ON NAVY SHIPS AND NAVAL BASES.

History of the Marine Corps

As a marine, my brother is part of one our country's oldest military organizations. The Marine Corps was formed on November 10, 1775, shortly before the American Revolution. Leaders of the colonial government felt a special group of soldiers was needed to **defend** the colonies on land and at sea.

Since then, the Marine Corps has fought in all major U.S. wars, from the Revolutionary War to today's **conflicts** in Iraq and Afghanistan. It's one of the country's most respected fighting forces. It's also the smallest. My brother is one of about 185,000 marines. He's proud to serve with such a special group.

THE MARINE CORPS GREW FROM MORE THAN 360 MARINES IN THE EARLY 1800S TO MORE THAN 200,000 BY 2010. IN RECENT YEARS, THE MARINE CORPS HAS GROWN SMALLER.

1864

2010

JOINING THE CORPS

All branches have requirements people must meet before joining. The Marine Corps is often seen as one of the toughest branches to join. First, you must be between 17 and 29 years old. My brother joined when he was 18. You have to be a U.S. citizen and you have to have a high school education.

All marines have to show that their body and mind are healthy. Finally, they take a test called the ASVAB. This test asks questions about science, math, and reading. It also asks questions about assembling objects and machines. My brother studied for a few weeks before taking the test. He was nervous!

MARINES HAVE TO THINK AND ACT QUICKLY. THE ASVAB TESTS THIS ABILITY. IT'S ALSO USED TO HELP MARINES CHOOSE A CAREER PATH AFTER THEY JOIN.

MILITARY MATTERS

My brother worked with a recruiter
before joining the marines. A recruiter
is a serviceman or servicewoman who
helps people choose to join the military.
My brother's recruiter answered the
questions our family had about what it's
like to join the marines.

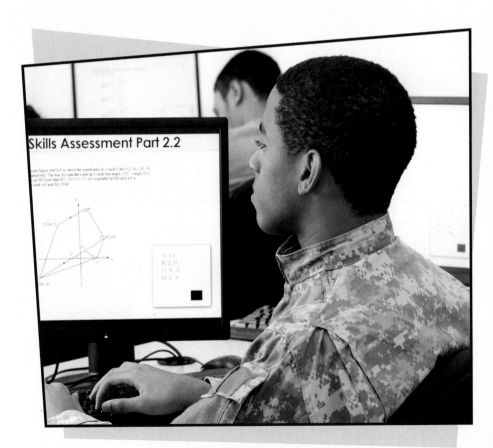

Going to Training

It was a big deal when my brother joined the Marine Corps. Being a marine is more than a full-time job—marines are always on duty, and they have to give up a lot in order to serve. That's one reason why I'm so proud of my brother.

After my brother **enlisted**, he went to basic training for 12 weeks. There are two places where marine **recruits** train: Parris Island in South Carolina and San Diego, California. My brother went to Parris Island. It's far from where we live, and I missed my brother a lot. Everyone in my family did.

★ ★ ★
Military Matters

Marine recruits from the West Coast train in San Diego, while recruits from the East Coast go to Parris Island. All female marines go to Parris Island.

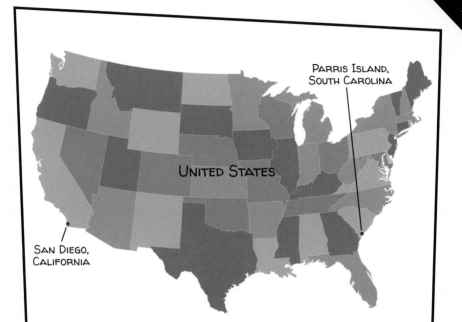

PARRIS ISLAND,
SOUTH CAROLINA

UNITED STATES

SAN DIEGO,
CALIFORNIA

IT WAS HARD TO SAY GOODBYE TO MY BROTHER WHEN HE LEFT FOR TRAINING, BUT I HAD TO BE STRONG. MY MOM SAID IT'S IMPORTANT TO SUPPORT OUR BROTHER. OUR SUPPORT AND LOVE HELPED HIM GET THROUGH TRAINING.

THE FEW, THE PROUD

When my brother arrived at training, he had to pass an Initial Strength Test (IST). He had to run 1.5 miles (2.4 km) in less than 13 and a half minutes, do 44 crunches in less than two minutes, and do two pull-ups.

That was just the beginning. Over 12 weeks, my brother went through training that tested his body and his mind. He did drills every day. He learned how to use **weapons** and how to fight hand to hand. He also learned **discipline** and teamwork. Above all, he learned the importance of honor and **loyalty**. My brother said his training was really hard, but it was worth it.

★★★
MILITARY MATTERS
"The Few, the Proud, the Marines" is a famous saying. It shows that becoming a marine is something only a small number of people experience.

MARINE TRAINING IS SOME OF THE HARDEST IN THE WORLD. MY FAMILY BELIEVED IN MY BROTHER, THOUGH. WE KNEW HE WAS STRONG AND **COMMITTED** TO BECOMING A MARINE.

My Brother Graduates

When my brother finished training, my family traveled to Parris Island to see him graduate. The day before graduation is called Family Day. It was the first time I saw my brother in 12 weeks! He showed us where he lived and trained, and we got to meet the people he trained with.

During graduation, my brother's drill sergeant, or leader, gave him the Marine Corps emblem. It's an eagle, globe, and anchor. Then, the drill sergeant called him a marine for the first time. My family was so proud of my brother. He was proud of himself, too.

MY PARENTS SAID MY BROTHER TRANSFORMED DURING TRAINING, WHICH MEANS HE CHANGED A LOT. I NOTICED IT, TOO! HE WAS STILL MY BROTHER, BUT NOW HE WAS ALSO A MARINE.

MILITARY MATTERS

An emblem is an object that acts as a
symbol for something. On the Marine Corps
emblem, the eagle, globe, and anchor stand
for the marines' commitment to protect
our nation's air, land, and sea.

A Career with the Marines

After graduation, my brother went to marines MOS school. MOS stands for "military occupational specialty." This is where he learned the skills needed for his military job. My brother is an engineer for the marines, so he learned how to build and repair roads and buildings. He also learned how to support marines while they're fighting on the ground.

There are many other jobs for marines, such as flying planes, driving tanks, and working on computers. Marines who know many languages can be translators, which are people who can express ideas in many languages. This is helpful in other countries. There are many careers within the Marine Corps.

★ ★ ★

Military Matters

Both men and women can join the marines, but as of 2015, women can't be in **combat**.

IN 2009, A SPECIAL GROUP OF FEMALE MARINES FORMED TO WORK WITH IRAQI WOMEN DURING OPERATION IRAQI FREEDOM. THEY WERE ABLE TO INTERACT WITH LOCAL WOMEN AND GIRLS, WHO OFTEN WEREN'T COMFORTABLE TALKING TO MALE SOLDIERS.

Semper Fi!

Marines can serve for a few years, or they can serve for their whole career. No matter how long they serve, they're marines for life. The Marine Corps has a saying that reminds them of that: "Semper Fidelis." This saying means "always faithful." Marines practice this saying every day, whether they're actively serving or not. I know my brother does!

Marines like my brother have given up a lot in order to protect our country. My family and other military families have given up a lot, too. Not many people can do what our brothers, sisters, moms, and dads do. They're our country's heroes.

GLOSSARY

combat: Fighting between armed forces.

committed: Feeling strongly tied to a cause, activity, or job.

conflict: A military fight.

crisis: A time of trouble or danger.

defend: To keep safe from harm.

discipline: Controlled behavior.

enlist: To join the armed services.

loyalty: A strong feeling of support.

naval base: A military base that is run by a country's navy.

protect: To keep safe.

rank: A person's position in the armed forces.

recruit: A person new to the armed forces who is not yet fully trained.

respond: To react to someone or something.

weapon: A tool made to cause harm.

INDEX

WEBSITES

Due to the changing nature of Internet links, PowerKids Press has developed an online list of websites related to the subject of this book. This site is updated regularly. Please use this link to access the list: www.powerkidslinks.com/mili/corp